Splendid Clientele . . .

Eric Walton

Be not afraid of greatness
Some are born great
Some achieve greatness
And some have greatness thrust upon them

- William Shakespeare

Discussion in a 100 Thousand Dollar Car

Driven by the will to breathe more
Much less the drive to succeed
More or less
Just make sure to proceed
Own my own terms in due time
Paid in full body work of art
Paid out of my own pocket
Owe myself this process to progress
Coast slow motion through my mind racing
Pacing myself
Placing myself to finish at the best speed
For better placement at the best table
Better placemats
Best wishes become better
Best believe
The better person cooks the best dishes
In the better place in mind with the best in mind
Food for thought for the best tastes
Mind you I remind you
A better tomorrow
At best today
The best always look for better
Forever…

Hold on… Who's this?
Let me stop this music…
Oh ok.
Just who I was trying to catch up with truth told
It's been a while…

Aye yo!

Oh wow! What up!
Here already?

Really?
It's been a while

                                                    Really?

Indeed

                                                    Time flies…

Whether you have fun or not

                                                    Indeed
                                          Have fun at least?

One can say but another can say the other.
You know how that goes.

                                                    Indeed

Long as my wings work, I can fly forever

                                              You forgot, B?

Absolutely not.
You asked the wrong question
More so thought the wrong answer

                                                    Word?

More so a letter

                                            You forgot, AB?

Now you asked another wrong question
Because you thought another wrong answer

                                                    Word?

Exactly

                                        You forgot a "be"?

Correct yet incorrect

                                                              I see

Now you C
Can't get from A to C without a B

                                                          Exactly
                                              You fly either way

Indeed
Hop in real quick

                                    I'm just going up the way

Yeah I know
Been there

                                                          Word?

Previously
Best believe I know where you're going

                                                            Bet

Already

                              So since you know where I'm going
                              Can you tell me something else?

Depending on what you need to know…

                                                    Is that right?

As ever…

                              Well you left before right there
                              Right when I was ready before…

Right
Left right there
You weren't ready

Couldn't afford the wait
Paying that much attention would cost me too much time

                                                    I see

What do you wish to know?
You recall…

                                        A lot of things…

Like?

                            Like I don't see myself half the time
                                It's like a full time thing

I see
It's a full time job

                            Doesn't make a lot of sense…

Actually makes a lot of sense

                                                Really?

Really

                                    Find your worth?
                        Cost so much time to pay attention?

Can't find what I never lost
I discovered what others never could see
Always knew the worth
Never knew why it went up and down
I found that eventually
That makes sense

                                        A lot of sense?

Exactly

                                        Ok cool

You don't know…
Like this:
You see what you are
You know what you know
Your issue:
How do you get to that point?
But to really keep it proper
How DID you get to that point?

                                        Exactly
                                        Right on

You hope for something you never known existed in an
existence
You already knew
Old becomes new
New becomes old
The store restores

                                        Damn!
                                        Right on

You're trying to take the perfect route
The proper steps
To get where you see
But you don't know how to get there
You don't recall
How can you recall something you never knew?
Especially when new is old
Start doubt
End panic
Every little step you take is a circle

                        Every step in a circle anyway

Exactly
You see

  Indeed

One of those where you know where you're going
You get to the point where you start to wonder if you get
where you end

                                                    Right on

Wrong thing to wonder
Wrong question again
Right answer though so right on
Wonder if it's all worth
It's there
It's not lost

                                                    Such as…

Seeing what you are supposed to be seeing
The depths of your seeing
You see up close?
You see far?
You see hopefulness?
You see happiness?
You see nothing last
First see forever…
Human nature sees nothing last
Nature sees forever first and last
A human sees in between and nothing else way too often

                                                    Indeed

Know what you see
See what you know
I see what you don't see
I know what you don't know
I have been where you see yourself going
I can even tell you what to see and what to know
One for sure, two for certain
One thing regardless of what I know…
It's still up to you to see and know…

                                                    …What SHOULD happen

My man. Right on…

                                        What should happen depends on…

Depends on what's right
Depends on that question you need to ask
You have the right answer
Ask the right question
Sounds like I'm being a jerk but…

                                                    Not the case
                                              I know and see you

Cool
Didn't think such
I know you better

                                                    Best believe…

Better yet since you did mention what should happen
You do see a pretty vantage point

                                                    I do huh…

Ever more…

                                        The bigger picture, huh…

Always and forever

                                        I know where I'm going
                                        But where do I come from?

You telling or asking?

                                        Seeing you've been there…

Has nothing to do with right now

Has nothing to do with right there
You see where you're going
You need to know something
You know already

                                                Yes

You asked me why
You asked me. Why?

                                        Oh my bad
                                        I didn't see

I know

                            I know where I'm going
                    But LORD where do I come from?

Right on
You're on the right path
You have to grasp what you ultimately see
You have to know yourself
See yourself besides yourself
Know where you stand
Have the proper vantage point and not the pretty one
Don't get too high. Don't get too low.
Be with the heights. Be humble for the depths.
The depths can be as great as the fall
We bring ourselves down
In turn we are lifted up
Know what to ask
See the journey
We can proceed soon after
Help yourself
Do the honors…

                    What is man that you are mindful of him,
                        And the son of man that You visit him?
                For You have made him a little lower than the angels,
                    And You have crowned him with glory and honor.

You have made him to have dominion over the works of
Your hands;
You have put all things under his feet.

Superbness
It's time…

If I knew then what I know now…

You just didn't see.
That's why I had to catch up.
You definitely cut the mustard
I'm glad
Let's move forward…

…and let the music play

Let the Music Play (Splendor)

Forever is a long time coming of age
Sentiments of a sage
Solomon's essays
Praise Splendor for days
Stay away in sanctuary caves for days
Like King Dave's
Wisdom defines between rulers and slaves
Words spoken and how one behaves
Behold what I've become
Mold the alphabet in the color of the sun
From day one
Make way for the marvelous
Sharpness
Never a dull moment
Riding dirty in a clean whip appeal to the masses
In any given matter
Solids
Liquids
Gasses
Set forth a stage to watch the plasma
Live viewing of a performance viewing life
Being pursued viewed
Under a microscope
Pursuing freedom or jail
My magnificence
Luxuriously rich
From everyone who paid interest
To those who pay attention
You pay me and I appreciated
Cook up a song with a divine wrist
Sublime lime twist
Sprinkled over fish
Wonderful dish
The Lord extended my wish
To redeem a supreme bliss
To ignorance I'm a terrorist
Feed the lambs

Water the grass
Green pastures alas
Food for thought
We baked the loaves fast
And fed the mass
Slow motion in the right lane
And let time pass
On the highway of life not in a hurry
It was moving too fast
Crash
Finally saw the light
Many colors through broken glass of shattered dreams…

Fabrics

Dressed superb in the finest fabrics
Lavish attributes living lavish in lavish habitats
Attributed to good practices
Eliminating bad habits
Up in the sky on cloud nine
On ten
Dancing on your ceiling
Very sure it's my floor
To my chagrin my grin blends more
With the sun shining bright
Through the reign
Celebrating as those seek shelter
I spill champagne
Sending love from above
As above, so below
Grow as God established
Hidden under covers extra mannish
Gorgeous glow of an aura
Tempura lobster euphoria
With the soul of a Harold's Chicken order

Yo yo yo… hold tight.
Stop the music right quick.

What gives?

Just wanted to expand on something
That came to mind as I wrote that…

As you wrote that?
The music playing?

Not the music per se but…
The bridge from A to C is B…
Best believe we'll soon enough
Cross it then

laughs I'm a sacrificial lamb now huh…

See that's why I roll with you...
You're a sharp cat
And lions are of the feline family
If I'm not mistaken

                          Iron sharpens iron from what I C...
                          Crossed that bridge already and...

Say it

                          Well it's like this...
                          From the lamb came the lion
                          Shocked a ton of people
                          Even myself...
                          But it's not like I didn't know it.

You just didn't C it.

                                              Indeed...

That's why I said cut the music
Let me let the mink drape for a minute

                          Read my mind...
                          You're superb with that

Indubitably

                                        Quote this...

Champagne in a plastic cup...

                                              laughs

The main issue with the world:
People took "Let Us make man in Our image"
Ran afoul with it

                  Adam was the beauty and glory of the universe...

Yet he came from dirt. Literally.
Formed from dirt
Dirtiest dude ever *laughs*
But yet…

He was in "Our image"

So here's the thing where the world messed up:
People became more focused on image rather than what
makes them
They became more focused on makeup rather than the make
up
Even being formed from dirt
Adam was formed from beauty…

Write

Last I checked B came before A
With that said
The very earth from which was a beautiful creation…
From jump

B comes before A?

You'll C soon enough…

You haven't been wrong so far

Image is everything now
Perception is reality
However those who choose to have the wrong perception
Rather they haven't fallen love to new depths
Can't fathom such an up close experience
They can't see past the image
They just roll with what they C
Their vision becomes you
Even worse
Their vision becomes your vision

Just take this for example:
I can pull up in this very $100K vehicle
This very one we're in right now
Hop out in a $3K tux
$100 roses falling at my feet for my very steps
People might think I'm beyond them
People might think I'm not one of them
People might think I'm not one to get my hands dirty

All of which isn't true…

Indubitably
However such is the state of mind
Not the state of grace

Precisely

Look at it this way:
James Bond wore a fly tux
Hopped out a $100K car
Aura like $100 roses
Many a marvelous woman
And was grimy
And would blow your head smooth off

laughs Man…

C…

Right on…

Look at Jordan
Everyone saw the shoes
The style
The superbness
No one sees the grit and grind
No one sees the make up until you see past that
Up close and personal
He was phenomenally fundamentally sound
Everyone saw the uniqueness

                                    People need to see the uniqueness…

Really they don't…

                                                              How so?

Self-preservation is the first law of nature…

                            Man what does THAT have to do with anything?

Nothing to do with anything
Something to do with everything
If you don't C yourself
Who will?

                                                              Oh sh…

People get wrapped up in the fabric
Totally ignoring the cloth

                                                              ICU

Very edge of death
Truth told
While living a lie…

                                                              Superbness

Look at it from my view above:
Moses was fresh to death
Living in Egyptian fabric
When he got covered in his cloth
From which he was truly cut…

                                                              Write on

King David was a shepherd
Regarded as a little lamb who fought lions
He became the lion who led the sheep
Absolutely didn't concern himself with the sheep…

Write on

King Solomon
Dressed in the finest fabrics
Lavish Attributes
Attributed to good practices
Due to the cloth from which he came
Asked for wisdom off the bat
With that…
He eliminated bad habits
When he abided by that very wisdom
This was all true
He did unwise
There the bad habits emerged
Submerged him
He got outside of self
Instead of besides self

Oh yeah…
King Solomon was grimy in the sense
Whacked his own brother
Trying to supplant his reign

Write on

I shall

Yes

Jesus Himself
The best
Not the best dressed
Many looked at Him super stupid
He was…

Say no more…

He fulfilled His duty to the fullest
Those seeking shelter from the reign…

                                        Covering their heads with ashes
                                               Trying not to get wet…

Let the champagne spill…

                                                              Oh!
                                        The champagne in the plastic cup!

Pour up…

                                               Let the mink drape…

I've always been extraordinary
Always had manners

                                               From extra mannish
                                           To extraordinary manners

Nothing new under the sun
Lord knows
I'm on cloud nine…

                                                       As above
                                                       So below

All I need to know
All I see…
Word to C

                                                       Refreshing

Shall we?

                                               Let the music play…

Vision of the Black Benz (My Intuition)

You know what's counterproductive...

I soon shall *laughs*

Seeking stability amongst instability

Right on

Discipline
Patience
Structure

Here's my question with that:
Rather with those...
When do you know when to say when?

When you truly listen to what is seen
When you finally see the white noise clearly

Remarkable

Resplendent actually

True

Too many times we let that guiding light become a
distraction
Rather than what it's truly there to be
We blind ourselves to chaos
We try to get order out of chaos
We then wonder why stability is within our grasp
Then it gets away so fast
It's like trying to grab the wind
The wind pushes you in whatever direction that blows

Indeed

I see you thinking

                              Well with the whole
                    Discipline, patience, and structure…

What about it…

                              Seeing what you are saying…
                    How do we actually those who need help?

Basically when do you know when to say when
More so
When do you see when to see when
When is it a loss to move…

                                        Exactly

Dude…
What does that have to do with anything
With them?
F them
We are taking a nature ride
In this luxurious automobile
And you are thinking of THEM?
You crazy?

                    But self-preservation is the first law…

Never Ignorant
Getting Goals
Accomplished

                              Pardon my disobedience

Don't trip on the lapse
This is why I caught you
On the second go round
Remember…

                              Yeah that's right

I'll even say this
You are right when you left them

                              You know I figured
                        I just have to live with regrets
                                    With that being
                        I truly don't regret sh…
                                 Well as far as…

Only regret:
It was done in the first place
You gave up your victory to run a race already won
Reason why you say "in the first place"
You were winning
Champagne was spilling
Someone wanted to celebrate themselves
They celebrate with you
Made it about themselves
All at your expense
Tears of joy quenched their thirsts
Made them better
My tears are champagne

                                          So on point

Told you
I've been here before

            So that's why I had the vision of the black Benz
                                         This is NICE
                            Saw the Dom P and all that

1996 to 2016
Nothing new under the sun
I don't care what time it is
Time heals
As the sun rejuvenates and replenishes
Through resplendence…
You see that…

                                        Indeed I do

Let me speak this...
Sometimes
The only way you have to bring clarity
Is letting them see you disappear
Really a lot of sometimes...

                        Absence makes the heart grow fonder?

More like absence makes one realize
What one has to see now...

                                        laughs

Like wiping chalk on a blackboard

                                        Provocative

Sit in a dark room
Suddenly
Someone flicks the light switch...

                                Speak your peace

Close the blinds to stop that beam of light
Only so you can't see the dust floating
That you didn't want to see...

                                State your grace

State of Grace

                                        My bad
                                        Right

Left that suddenly when we made the left turn
Right there...

                                Indeed so...

If you don't see the best yourself
Then how in the world
Can you see the universe…

Celestial…

Bask in the glory

Dope on the Table (72 Ounces)

What never was imagined
Was the image
Right in front of the eyes wide shut
Sadly these people never truly though you were dope enough
Oddly enough
If you acted like a dope
They thought you were very dope
Would tell you to stay dope
But you couldn't be the best dope
Constantly stepped on
Used as a stepping stone
Elevating themselves as they stepped over you
Stretch you out using you to get higher
Lift them up so they can be above you
Ultimately getting over on you
Fly in the friendly sky
Without leaving the ground
Head in the clouds
Never leaving the ground
But you can't tell them different
They all look the same
But look at you different
Soon as they come down they realize how much they needed
you
Never enough how they used you
It's all dope in their clouded vision
They get a peek where you stand
They wish to enjoy
Little do they know
They belittle the wisdom trying to peak at what they're never
blessed to see
They never see the table
Never sat with the pure uncut
Mind numbing
Dope on the Table
Being prepared for distribution
72 Ounces

2 keys to open doors
To travel and the mind can be free
Instead of being a prisoner in their ways
Always in jail never seeing the confinement
Stuck in a way of thinking inside the cell
The nucleus of everything revolves around it
Never considering life outside
Never considering their ceiling is your floor
The best they see
The worst you know…

Be very cognizant whom you extend a helping hand
The same hand to help pull someone up
The same hand allows someone to pull you down

The saying goes
"It's lonely at the top"
Here's why this is confusing:
Being at the top doesn't mean that you suffer from success
Nor does it mean that you by yourself are lonely
The lonely often runs in packs
Wolves simply waiting to devour the sheep
The very sheep that cries wolf in some cases

The wisest is the richest
Never give away your riches to those poor in spirit
Those always scheming for riches
They live a fast life
Dying to get rich without any effort
So when you give riches to those
You lose your value
Giving yourself away for nothing

So pay attention
Spend time to become more valuable
More aware
Better this than to cost your life
Invest in self
Bet on self
All it takes is 72 ounces

2 keys of life to open any possibility
Dope on the Table

More than anyone could imagine
The very image in front of those eyes wide shut to see

Champagne in a Plastic Cup (My Influence)

Realizing the realism of life and actuality
It's sad to see people define themselves by salary
Casual conversation can turn into a casualty
The fallacy of jealousy plus envy equals tragedy
Mathematically
Majesty of one turns many into serial killers magically
Tricked by what they see you in and what they see you as
naturally
Spirited competition exists when you're truly unaware
actually
Their opinions of you somehow become matter of factually

Turn this sh… off…

My Masterpiece

Let me ask you something

Go ahead

I'm sure you have an idea what I'm going to ask

50/50 chance with everything in life…

How do you deal with
The loneliness of being in such a different space

Master peace

How so?

First and foremost
You have to know the difference
Between lonely and loner
Next is to understand

So what's the difference?

Since you asked…
The lonely runs in packs
The loner stands still

I don't understand

You ever wonder how people can sit around
Do the same things for months at a time

Yeah

Even at the expense of not wanting anything else
Even worse
Not wanting to know anything else…

I've noticed that but…

You didn't see it

Indeed

Well…
That's the tell-tale of a lonely heart

But…
Oh.
The good old
"Misery loves company"

Precisely

OK
I see now

The thing that can cause an issue:
Being around lonely people
Not having a clue they're entertaining their misery
With your company
That can stagnate you in so many ways
Ultimately lead you down to that lower level we all should avoid
Sadly enough…
These people are very much comfortable with having
Hell of a time

As I've learned…

You already know…

Ultimately discovered

The great Muhammad Ali:
The man who views the world at 50
The same as he did at 20…

...has wasted 30 years of his life

It's all mathematics

Life science

And mathematics is the science of numbers

Yet that's everything
Patterns of numbers
Tell all we need to know...

...and we all must understand

...and see for ourselves

You see it clearly

So the loner stands still
To notice all of this
With this he's never lonely
Simply because...

Or she

Right...
He or she is never lonely
Simply because
One is truly never alone
When it comes to growth
You have to be involved with self
Then see outside of self
There's a maddening process

Which is why...
If you get besides self
Then truly one should be adjacent to greatness
The greatness of self
Leads to the brilliance that shines forth
How can one be brilliant

If there's no one else to see the shine

                              Great minds think alike
                              Brilliance is of one

Only the sun shines through the entire universe
Even when we don't see it…

                              We know it's still there
                                        Still…

Bingo bango
The light bulb just bulbed
laughs

                                        Indeed it has

The loner stands still
The sun isn't going anywhere
Either you come to it
Or you go away from it…
You don't want it to shine so tough on you
You go for shade
You stay in the house
Heck you can cover the windows
Better yet…

                                        Run for cover

The lonely runs in packs
They cover their misery with the company they keep
No wishes to stand out
Just be comfortable in running with each other
Just running from problems…

                                        Right

But like I said earlier
You have to have some self-awareness of greatness
To see outside of yourself

Get mad in some form
Get besides yourself
When you're mad, the clock ticks

What if you never hear it?

You will eventually
Silence is golden
You can see sounds and hear sights

Damn
What if the clock has no batteries?

The earth still spins
The sun still shines tomorrow

There's that "still" sh... again

laughs

If you don't hear it
Then you don't want to see

Thus "you will eventually"
If animals can adjust to nature naturally...
Naturally Adam named every single animal in nature...

Right

Your environment can dictate a lot to you
Also hinder you

So it's indeed something else
That supersedes the environment...

Glad we're past the point of you asking

Thanks

You just forgot what you know

Really you've tried to forget what you know
In a few cases

                                        More like bottles…

laughs

                                        Laugh now
                                        Cry later

Tears of joy

                                        Definitely
                                        Many a meaning

Wish I could've shed light
Instead of shed tears
But…

                    Proper preparation prevents poor performance

Right over left

                                        Aid and assist…
                        You did just that with this ride
                        What a luxurious ride at that
                        You've helped a whole lot
                        Served a lot of justice
                        I didn't see it but…

The fact that you knew it was proper preparation
The perspective increases as your growth:
If you need to see farther
Then you need to go higher
How can you get higher unless you build your foundation
Then build upon the foundation

                                    And that constant elevation
                                    Prevents poor performance…

Every little step you take
Take your best foot forward
Right over left…

                                       Write history as you go…

Right history as you go
We can change it
We shouldn't want to change it
Sure it's things we should want to do different
Things we want to change as far as our approach
But…

                          We didn't see it for what it was
                              Let alone see it clearly
                            Because our perspective…

Aid and assist

                                             But I did
                                    Yet I didn't…

Self-preservation is the first law of nature

                                           True
                                  sheds tears

Let the champagne spill
Nothing messy about that at all

                                       You already know

Becoming a slave to the rhythm of your heartbeat
You create the master peace…
The hardest work…
The reason you are becoming king
Don't hear anything else
Just hear self
The heart is the engine that pumps life throughout

And if no one else hears your heart…

But they have to see it
Because they hear their own
Lord knows we all beat to a different drum

So it's about being in tune with one another

You have to have someone help you get in tune with a
musical instrument do you not…

Aid and assist

If the harmony isn't there
Then how can you beautiful music be created…
Otherwise it's just noise not sound

Noise is a type of sound

You can say a lot and say nothing

Yet silence is golden…

Going gold is 500 Thousand sold
laughs

laughs
Well said

Indubitably

So…. Keep you in check?

My Master… Peace

Fly and Wonderful

Definitely not the Word to play…

Oh so I've learned…

Tense

                                        Very… I learn

My man…

                I never saw peace like that for a long time coming…
                        I never saw peace like that forever…
                I always saw strength as a means to get comfort
                                        Having to be strong
                                In order to be strong for others
                                        At my weakest point
                        Never being one to reveal my weak spot
                                That alone made me weak
                                        Because…

Took so much strength
Hiding a weakness…

                                                        Right

Merely a deficiency

                                        I see that now but…

Others dictated it for you

                                        Based on their vision

Their perspective was rather shallow

                                                        Very

Growth and Development

                                        The Shield of David

The Star of David

                                          Same difference

Perspective is power

                    Thus the relevance of seeing something different
                              Is the same thing as you get older

Nothing new under the sun…

                                        The same sun that stands still

No matter where you run
It will be there

                    And so will the very things you will need to progress
                                        From truth told…

The lonely runs in packs

                                        The loner stands still

We're almost there

                                                    Right on

$100 Roses

Presented in the present tense
From past events
Future has you all bent out of shape
From your escape
Much rather your return a place
Less traveled but you've been there
100 times over
$100 Roses
Planted at your feet
Cultivated and grown
From a place of uniqueness
Why live in the background
Until you're back ground
Sound choices
Found voices
Lost in translation
In transition
From a long day
1000 times over
Short term memories go a long way
Forget what you know
Know what is forgotten
You're fresh to death
Spoiled rotten
You're not being obnoxious
Vision of the Black Benz
The woman of your dreams
Everyone sleep walking
Know what time it is
Time peace stands still
Thoughts of Ralph Lauren watches
While living out your dreams
Wide awake
Luxury homes
Match made in heaven
Sparkling flames
Fire and desire

Acquire tastes
Quench thirsts with love
Divine charity
Given the opportunity
To see yourself
Be yourself
Just how you saw yourself
Saw your wealth
Before you see it
Ideally you can't grasp it
Reality is more like you can't grasp it
Behold what I be
Hold
I came from many a places
Different times
Same statements of greatness
Written in the sky
Prize worthy
Worthy of praise
Displayed with the ribbon
Type words of glory
Stories of amazement
With a background that amazes
And a teammate that's amazing
Together
Before meeting
Come together
Common accord
Working together
In a harmony
Greeting the masses
Supreme confidence
Self-esteem something else
Super
Superb
Supreme
Confidence speaks itself
Comfort in help
Come forth
Plead the fifth

On the third day
The two became one
Not a second later
First thought was get it together
Separate from the nonsense
Let my conscience be free
Prisoner of being ahead of my time
And everyone else
The marvelous makes way
A soundtrack for others to follow
You can have it for yourselves
Though I suggest that you borrow
I want it back
After you gain interest and pay attention

A midsummer night's dream
Gives way to being wide awake
Come tomorrow…

Champagne Thought Incomplete

Road to glory
Glorious story
Notorious told me
Sky's the limit
Felt limited
By such a high standard
Granted I'm grounded
I would rather see far beyond
Live limitless
Beyond the horizon
Beyond clear sense of reality
Saw much further
Into a different galaxy
Star struck
Awe struck
By a beautiful being
Seeing a dream
Wide awake
How many walks of life would I make
Recapture the beauty beheld
For Heaven's sake
Held part of me away
Close by
Near and dear…

Superbness Pt. Forever...

You never go through life without owing
Someone
Something…

                             As I'm very well aware

As you should

                             This very trip itself
                             I appreciate you for this
                             I owe that to you

We owe it to self

                             Indeed

I look at it like this:
You owe the next person
The very time it took to create the world

                             Word?

Indubitably

                             Connect the dots
                             Build the bridge…

"Let Us make man in Our image"

                             Yeah I figured that…

The Golden Rule

                             What about it?

That's all you need to know

                                        Let the mink drape

The Golden Rule
Be worth your weight in gold
Silence is golden

                                        What's understood
                                        Needs not be said

The only thing you need to see:
Each other…

                                        That's impeccable

The things that we forever shall owe:
Acknowledgement that the person is a human being
Love that you have for self is owed to the next person
Respect owed is saying everything with actions, never words

                                        And then there was…

And forever it is…

Welp… you are now here

                                        Wow
                                        Always had this in mind
                                        Truly did
                                        Never knew how to get here
                                        Then you came along
                                        In time…

Time heals wounds

                                        Right
                                        I shall see you later
                                        Thanks for the ride...

I'll leave on this note:

The very blood in the body is blue
The very air we breathe can't be seen
Yet that which is colorless makes the blood red
The same God we can't see is indeed the same God that:
Gave us life, has given us Life, gives us life
Life happens in threes
I said it back then when I was cloudy
It is seen clearly as I stand
Majestic royalty was always in my veins
The color purple showing I am king
Self
Lord
Master
Green my growth
Gold my riches and shine
Together formed the crown of wisdom
Blood shed for all to see
Took my breath away along with everyone else…

The higher you go in elevation
As it pertains the earth
You have more trouble breathing
The air runs out
However the nature of God is not the nature of man
God gave me life the higher I elevated
He blew breath in my lungs
A breath of fresh air with every ascent
He brought me to my rightful place
Standing on cloud nine
Taking each step forward to reach another cloud
Then another
Until I was all alone
Until I had my proper perspective
Truly staying above everyone and everything
Not bringing myself down to those wanting company
Not lowering myself to those unwilling to grow
Maintain constant elevation

I'm in a rarified air being a rare heir
I've been here before

I had to bet on myself
I had to remind myself
I had to ride with myself
I had to talk with myself
I had to trust myself

Splendid Clientele...

I'm so far ahead of my time
I'm 'bout to start another life
Look behind you
I'm 'bout to pass you twice
Back to the future
Gotta slow up for the present
I'm fast
N…s can't get past my past…

- Shawn "Jay Z" Carter

Splendid Clientele
(E. Walton)

Discussions in a 100 Thousand Dollar Car

Let the Music Play (Splendor)

Fabrics

Vision of the Black Benz (My Intuition)

Dope on the Table (72 Ounces)

Champagne in a Plastic Cup (My Influence)

My Masterpiece

$100 Roses

Champagne Thought Incomplete

Superbness Pt. Forever...

Please feel free to buy my previous works of art.

These are readily available online, preferably
Createspace.com and Amazon.com.

Physical copies definitely can be made available upon
demand and notice.

These works of art are the foundation and shall give further
clarity to the concepts in which this particular work of art,
Splendid Clientele, you have just completed.

Each book represents a concept and gained understanding.
Each book follows a certain path based off of one another.

Support the arts!

Works of Art:

The Rise with Love: Eric Walton in Rare Art Form
(The Blue Book)

Splendid State of Mind
(The Purple Book)

Thank You